A FOUNDATION

THE GOSPEL OF MARK

With additional material by Steve Legg

TODAY'S
N·I·V

Hodder & Stoughton
LONDON SYDNEY AUCKLAND

'You Christians have in your keeping a document with enough dynamite in it to blow the whole of civilisation to bits; to turn the world upside-down; to bring peace to this war-torn world. But you read it as if it were just good literature, and nothing else.'

MAHATMA GANDHI

BUILT TO LAST

by Steve Legg

I saw an advert on the side of a van that made me chuckle. The proprietors of the building firm were called "Singh and Singh" and underneath their name had the slogan "You've had the Cowboys now hire the Indians!"

Jesus probably knew most of the cowboy builders in the Palestine building trade, having spent most of his working life grafting away on the building site. He would have been genned up on all the tricks of the trade and knew all the shortcuts. He certainly knew that one of the keys to a really good building was the need for strong foundations. This is a story he told one day that was probably inspired by an actual building site he'd been working on:

"Why do you call me, 'Lord, Lord,' and do not do what I say? As for those who come to me and hear my words and put them into practice, I will show you what they are like. They are like a man building a house, who dug down deep and laid the foundation on rock. When the flood came, the torrent struck that house but could not shake it, because it was well built. But those who hear my words and do not put them into practice are like a man who built a house on the ground without a foundation. The moment the torrent struck that house, it collapsed and its destruction was complete." (Luke 6:46–9)

Like so many people the foolish man wanted the easy way out. The thought of digging into rock probably made him sweat just thinking about it. The sand was a much nicer proposition and much less trouble. If I'm really honest, there are easier ways to live than the Christian way. It's certainly not the cushy, simple option. In fact, being a Christian is in many respects very difficult, but Jesus' way is the best way and ultimately good foundations will help it stand the test of time.

It could be that you need to re-point your foundations which have not really received much care and attention for years. For others the foundations might have got flooded and be in danger of subsidence, so it'll be time to pump out what's not needed and set yourself on really solid ground all over again. For brand new Christians you'll be starting from scratch so make your foundations strong, your floors flat and your walls straight and you'll stand firm for the coming years.

Whichever category you fit into, the book you have in your hand will help. It's part of the Bible, and is a biography written by a man named Mark. He was an eyewitness to the remarkable events that occurred in a part of the Roman Empire some two thousand years ago. His book is fast-moving and packed full of action and drama. Mark tells the story of the most extraordinary man to have ever walked the face of the earth. A man who changed the world. A man from whose birth the very years are dated. A man who was born in poverty and died like a common criminal, yet here and now in the 21st century more than 1.5 billion men, women and children follow him. This man is Jesus and he wants to get to know you.

PROLOGUE

Joseph accepts Jesus as his son

This is how the birth of Jesus Christ came about: His mother Mary was pledged to be married to Joseph, but before they came together, she was found to be pregnant through the Holy Spirit. Because Joseph her husband was a righteous man and did not want to expose her to public disgrace, he had in mind to divorce her quietly.

But after he had considered this, an angel of the Lord appeared to him in a dream and said, "Joseph son of David, do not be afraid to take Mary home as your wife, because what is conceived in her is from the Holy Spirit. She will give birth to a son, and you are to give him the name Jesus, because he will save his people from their sins."

All this took place to fulfil what the Lord had said through the prophet: "The virgin will conceive and give birth to a son, and they will call him Immanuel" – which means, "God with us."

When Joseph woke up, he did what the angel of the Lord had commanded him and took Mary home as his wife. But he had no union with her until she gave birth to a son. And he gave him the name Jesus.

FROM THE GOSPEL OF MATTHEW 1:18–25

**The Birth of Jesus
(Matthew 1:18–25)**

In 1996, American Rock singer Joan Osborne's song "One of Us" was in the charts for weeks, with some interesting lyrics. "What if God was one of us? Just a slob like one of us." I'm sure many religious people were offended by the insinuation that God was a slob. But she was making a very important point, and that's what the first Christmas was all about – that God left the splendour of heaven and came in flesh and blood to live with us for a while, in the form of Jesus.

3

The birth of Jesus

In those days Caesar Augustus issued a decree that a census should be taken of the entire Roman world. (This was the first census that took place while Quirinius was governor of Syria.) And everyone went to their own town to register.

So Joseph also went up from the town of Nazareth in Galilee to Judea, to Bethlehem the town of David, because he belonged to the house and line of David. He went there to register with Mary, who was pledged to be married to him and was expecting a child. While they were there, the time came for the baby to be born, and she gave birth to her firstborn, a son. She wrapped him in cloths and placed him in a manger, because there was no guest room available for them.

The shepherds and the angels

And there were shepherds living out in the fields nearby, keeping watch over their flocks at night. An angel of the Lord appeared to them, and the glory of the Lord shone around them, and they were terrified. But the angel said to them, "Do not be afraid. I bring you good news of great joy that will be for all the people. Today in the town of David a Saviour has been born to you; he is the Messiah, the Lord. This will be a sign to you: You will find a baby wrapped in cloths and lying in a manger."

Suddenly a great company of the heavenly host appeared with the angel, praising God and saying,

> *"Glory to God in the highest heaven,*
> *and on earth peace to those on whom his favour rests."*

When the angels had left them and gone into heaven, the shepherds said to one another, "Let's go to Bethlehem and see this thing that has happened, which the Lord has told us about."

So they hurried off and found Mary and Joseph, and the baby, who was lying in the manger. When they had seen him, they spread the word concerning what had been told them about this child, and all who heard it were amazed at what the shepherds said to them. But Mary treasured up all these things and pondered them in her heart. The shepherds returned, glorifying and praising God for all the things they had heard and seen, which were just as they had been told.

FROM THE GOSPEL OF LUKE 2:1–20

The Magi visit the Messiah

After Jesus was born in Bethlehem in Judea, during the time of King Herod, Magi from the east came to Jerusalem and asked, "Where is the one who has been born king of the Jews? We saw his star when it rose and have come to worship him."

When King Herod heard this he was disturbed, and all Jerusalem with him. When he had called together all the people's chief priests and teachers of the law, he asked them where the Messiah was to be born. "In Bethlehem in Judea," they replied, "for this is what the prophet has written:

> "'But you, Bethlehem, in the
>   land of Judah,
> are by no means least among
>   the rulers of Judah;
> for out of you will come a ruler
>   who will be the shepherd of my
>   people Israel.'"

Then Herod called the Magi secretly and found out from them the exact

---

Magi (Matthew 2:1–12)
It was probably two years after Jesus was born that the Magi arrived with their expensive presents. They weren't kings, they were actually non-Jewish astronomers and astrologers, and there probably weren't three of them. Some sources suggest that there were as many as a hundred of these wise men. I have to admit, it would make a cracking Christmas play!

time the star had appeared. He sent them to Bethlehem and said, "Go and make a careful search for the child. As soon as you find him, report to me, so that I too may go and worship him."

After they had heard the king, they went on their way, and the star they had seen when it rose went ahead of them until it stopped over the place where the child was. When they saw the star, they were overjoyed. On coming to the house, they saw the child with his mother Mary, and they bowed down and worshipped him. Then they opened their treasures and presented him with gifts of gold, frankincense and myrrh. And having been warned in a dream not to go back to Herod, they returned to their country by another route.

The escape to Egypt

When they had gone, an angel of the Lord appeared to Joseph in a dream. "Get up," he said, "take the child and his mother and escape to Egypt. Stay there until I tell you, for Herod is going to search for the child to kill him."

So he got up, took the child and his mother during the night and left for Egypt, where he stayed until the death of Herod. And so was fulfilled what the Lord had said through the prophet: "Out of Egypt I called my son."

When Herod realised that he had been outwitted by the Magi, he was furious, and he gave orders to kill all the boys in Bethlehem and its vicinity

---

Escape to Egypt
(Matthew 2:13–18)

Palestine at the time was controlled by Herod the Great, a powerful king who was driven insane through his fear of treachery. He was so paranoid he murdered his wife Mariamne, his mother-in-law (no funny comments please!) and his sons Alexander, Aristobulus and Antipater. Rumours of a rival king of the Jews, Jesus, sparked off Herod's paranoia all over again. He tried to have the baby Jesus murdered. God, however, had other plans . . .

who were two years old and under, in accordance with the time he had learned from the Magi. Then what was said through the prophet Jeremiah was fulfilled:

"A voice is heard in Ramah,
weeping and great mourning,
Rachel weeping for her children
and refusing to be comforted,
because they are no more."

The return to Nazareth

After Herod died, an angel of the Lord appeared in a dream to Joseph in Egypt and said, "Get up, take the child and his mother and go to the land of Israel, for those who were trying to take the child's life are dead."

So he got up, took the child and his mother and went to the land of Israel. But when he heard that Archelaus was reigning in Judea in place of his father Herod, he was afraid to go there. Having been warned in a dream, he withdrew to the district of Galilee, and he went and lived in a town called Nazareth. So was fulfilled what was said through the prophets: "He will be called a Nazarene."

FROM THE GOSPEL OF MATTHEW 2:1–23

MARK

John the Baptist prepares the way

The beginning of the good news about Jesus the Messiah,

as it is written in Isaiah the prophet:

"I will send my messenger ahead of you,
who will prepare your way" –
"a voice of one calling in the desert,
'Prepare the way for the Lord,
make straight paths for him.' "

And so John the Baptist appeared in the desert region, preaching a baptism of repentance for the forgiveness of sins. The whole Judean countryside and all the people of Jerusalem went out to him. Confessing their sins, they were baptised by him in the River Jordan. John wore clothing made of camel's hair, with a leather belt round his waist, and he ate locusts and wild honey. And this was his message: "After me comes the one more powerful than I, the thongs of whose sandals I am not worthy to stoop down and untie. I baptise you with water, but he will baptise you with the Holy Spirit."

The baptism and testing of Jesus

At that time Jesus came from Nazareth in Galilee and was baptised by John in the Jordan. Just as Jesus was coming up out of the water, he saw heaven being torn open and the Spirit descending on him like a dove. And a voice came from heaven: "You are my Son, whom I love; with you I am well pleased."

> **John the Baptist (Mark 1:1–8)**
> John the Baptist was Jesus' cousin and a fiery and unconventional preacher. He spoke about the need to "repent" to be forgiven. The word "repentance" means a turning away from wrong and going in a new direction.

At once the Spirit sent him out into the desert, and he was in the desert for forty days, being tempted by Satan. He was with the wild animals, and angels attended him.

Jesus announces the good news

After John was put in prison, Jesus went into Galilee, proclaiming the good news of God. "The time has come," he said. "The kingdom of God has come near. Repent and believe the good news!"

Jesus calls his first disciples

As Jesus walked beside the Sea of Galilee, he saw Simon and his brother Andrew casting a net into the lake, for they were fishermen. "Come, follow me," Jesus said, "and I will send you out to catch people." At once they left their nets and followed him.

When he had gone a little farther, he saw James son of Zebedee and his brother John in a boat, preparing their nets. Without delay he called them, and they left their father Zebedee in the boat with the hired men and followed him.

Jesus drives out an evil spirit

They went to Capernaum, and when the Sabbath came, Jesus went into the synagogue and began to teach. The people were amazed at his teaching, because he taught them as one who had authority, not as the teachers of the law. Just then a man in their synagogue who was possessed by an evil spirit cried out, "What do you want with us, Jesus of Nazareth? Have you come to destroy us? I know who you are – the Holy One of God!"

"Be quiet!" said Jesus sternly. "Come out of him!" The evil spirit shook the man violently and came out of him with a shriek.

The people were all so amazed that they asked each other, "What is this? A new teaching – and with authority! He even gives orders to evil spirits and they obey him." News about him spread quickly over the whole region of Galilee.

Jesus heals many

As soon as they left the synagogue, they went with James and John to the home of Simon and Andrew. Simon's mother-in-law was in bed with a fever, and they immediately told Jesus about her. So he went to her, took her hand and helped her up. The fever left her and she began to wait on them.

That evening after sunset the people brought to Jesus all who were ill and demon-possessed. The whole town gathered at the door, and Jesus healed many who had various diseases. He also drove out many demons, but he would not let the demons speak because they knew who he was.

Jesus prays in a solitary place

Very early in the morning, while it was still dark, Jesus got up, left the house and went off to a solitary place, where he prayed. Simon and his companions went to look for him, and when they found him, they exclaimed: "Everyone is looking for you!"

Jesus replied, "Let us go somewhere else – to the nearby villages – so that I can preach there also. That is why I have come." So he travelled throughout Galilee, preaching in their synagogues and driving out demons.

Healing (Mark 1:29–34)

Healing was part and parcel of Jesus' life and work. Christians believe that his power to heal is still around today. For example, the New Life Christian Centre in Argentina has grown from 100 people in 1982 to around 12,000 people in May 2001. The church sees some 200 people become Christians every week. The children and teenagers regularly visit the children's hospital to pray for young patients there, with staggering results such as AIDS-infected babies being healed. In fact there have been so many miracles that the church has its own "department of miracles" with a doctor working to verify the healings.

Jesus heals a man with leprosy

A man with leprosy came to him and begged him on his knees, "If you are willing, you can make me clean."

Jesus was indignant. He reached out his hand and touched the man. "I am willing," he said. "Be clean!" Immediately the leprosy left him and he was cleansed.

Jesus sent him away at once with a strong warning: "See that you don't tell this to anyone. But go, show yourself to the priest and offer the sacrifices that Moses commanded for your cleansing, as a testimony to them." Instead he went out and began to talk freely, spreading the news. As a result, Jesus could no longer enter a town openly but stayed outside in lonely places. Yet the people still came to him from everywhere.

Jesus forgives and heals a paralysed man

A few days later, when Jesus again entered Capernaum, the people heard that he had come home. So many gathered that there was no room left, not even outside the door, and he preached the word to them. Some men came, bringing to him a paralysed man, carried by four of them. Since they could not get him to Jesus because of the crowd, they made an opening in the roof above Jesus by digging through it and then lowered the mat the man was lying on. When Jesus saw their faith, he said to the paralysed man, "Son, your sins are forgiven."

Now some teachers of the law were sitting there, thinking to themselves, "Why does this fellow talk like that? He's blaspheming! Who can forgive sins but God alone?"

Immediately Jesus knew in his spirit that this was what they were thinking in their hearts, and he said to them, "Why are you thinking these things? 'Which is easier: to say to this paralysed man, 'Your sins are forgiven,' or to say, 'Get up, take your mat and walk'? But I want you to know that the Son of Man has authority on earth to forgive sins." So he said to the man, "I tell you, get up, take your mat and go home." He got up, took his mat and walked out in full view of them all. This amazed everyone and they praised God, saying, "We have never seen anything like this!"

Jesus calls Levi and eats with sinners

Once again Jesus went out beside the lake. A large crowd came to him, and he began to teach them. As he walked along, he saw Levi son of Alphaeus sitting at the tax collector's booth. "Follow me," Jesus told him, and Levi got up and followed him.

While Jesus was having dinner at Levi's house, many tax collectors and "sinners" were eating with him and his disciples, for there were many who followed him. When the teachers of the law who were Pharisees saw him eating with the "sinners" and tax collectors, they asked his disciples: "Why does he eat with tax collectors and 'sinners'?"

On hearing this, Jesus said to them, "It is not the healthy who need a doctor, but those who are ill. I have not come to call the righteous, but sinners."

Jesus questioned about fasting

Now John's disciples and the Pharisees were fasting. Some people came and asked Jesus, "How is it that John's disciples and the disciples of the Pharisees are fasting, but yours are not?"

Jesus answered, "How can the guests of the bridegroom fast while he is with them? They cannot, so long as they have him with them. But the time will come when the bridegroom will be taken from them, and on that day they will fast.

"No-one sews a patch of unshrunk cloth on an old garment. If they do, the new piece will pull away from the old, making the tear worse. And people do not pour new wine into old wineskins. If they do, the wine will burst the skins, and both the wine and the wineskins will be ruined. No, they pour new wine into new wineskins."

Jesus is Lord of the Sabbath

One Sabbath Jesus was going through the cornfields, and as his disciples walked along, they began to pick some ears of corn. The Pharisees said to him, "Look, why are they doing what is unlawful on the Sabbath?"

He answered, "Have you never read what David did when he and his companions were hungry and in need? In the days of Abiathar the high priest, he entered the house of God and ate the consecrated bread, which is lawful only for priests to eat. And he also gave some to his companions."

Then he said to them, "The Sabbath was made for people, not people for the Sabbath. So the Son of Man is Lord even of the Sabbath."

Jesus heals on the Sabbath

Another time he went into the synagogue, and a man with a shrivelled hand was there. Some of them were looking for a reason to accuse Jesus, so they watched him closely to see if he would heal him on the Sabbath. Jesus said to the man with the shrivelled hand, "Stand up in front of everyone."

Then Jesus asked them, "Which is lawful on the Sabbath: to do good or to do evil, to save life or to kill?" But they remained silent.

He looked around at them in anger and, deeply distressed at their stubborn hearts, said to the man, "Stretch out your hand." He stretched it out, and his hand was completely restored. Then the

> **Sabbath (Mark 2:23–3:6)**
> "Sabbath" actually means "rest". In Jesus' day the Sabbath day was Saturday, the seventh and last day of the Jewish week, when Jews worshipped God. A great idea in principle, until the religious authorities added loads of rules and regulations, in fact they listed thirty-nine types of activities banned on the Sabbath! The Church eventually decided to make Sunday the Sabbath to remember the day that Jesus rose from the dead.

Pharisees went out and began to plot with the Herodians how they might kill Jesus.

Crowds follow Jesus

Jesus withdrew with his disciples to the lake, and a large crowd from Galilee followed. When they heard all he was doing, many people came to him from Judea, Jerusalem, Idumea, and the regions across the Jordan and around Tyre and Sidon. Because of the crowd he told his disciples to have a small boat ready for him, to keep the people from crowding him. For he had healed many, so that those with diseases were pushing forward to touch him. Whenever the evil spirits saw him, they fell down before him and cried out, "You are the Son of God." But he gave them strict orders not to tell others about him.

Jesus appoints the Twelve

Jesus went up on a mountainside and called to him those he wanted, and they came to him. He appointed twelve that they might be with him and that he might send them out to preach and to have authority to drive out demons. These are the twelve he appointed: Simon (to whom he gave the name Peter); James son of Zebedee and his brother John (to them he gave the name Boanerges, which means Sons of Thunder); Andrew, Philip, Bartholomew, Matthew, Thomas, James son of Alphaeus, Thaddaeus, Simon the Zealot and Judas Iscariot, who betrayed him.

Jesus accused by his family and by teachers of the law

Then Jesus entered a house, and again a crowd gathered, so that he and his disciples were not even able to eat. When his family heard about this, they went to take charge of him, for they said, "He is out of his mind."

And the teachers of the law who came down from Jerusalem said, "He is possessed by Beelzebul! By the prince of demons he is driving out demons."

So Jesus called them over to him and began to speak to them in parables: "How can Satan drive out Satan? If a kingdom is divided against itself, that kingdom cannot stand. If a house is divided against itself, that house cannot stand. And if Satan opposes himself and is divided, he cannot stand; his end has come. In fact, no-one can enter a strong man's house without first tying him up. Then he can plunder the strong man's house. Truly I tell you, people will be forgiven all their sins and all the blasphemies they utter. But whoever blasphemes against the Holy Spirit will never be forgiven, but is guilty of an eternal sin."

He said this because they were saying, "He has an evil spirit."

Then Jesus' mother and brothers arrived. Standing outside, they sent someone in to call him. A crowd was sitting round him, and they told him, "Your mother and brothers are outside looking for you."

"Who are my mother and my brothers?" he asked.

Then he looked at those seated in a circle round him and said, "Here are my mother and my brothers! Whoever does God's will is my brother and sister and mother."

Parables (Mark 4:1–34)

Jesus often used parables – stories that ordinary people would understand. If he were around today he would probably tell parables about Eastenders, PlayStation and the Internet. He used these stories to make the truth easier to understand and harder to forget.

The parable of the sower

Again Jesus began to teach by the lake. The crowd that gathered round him was so large that he got into a boat and sat in it out on the lake, while all the people were along the shore at the water's edge. He taught them many things by parables, and in his teaching said: "Listen! A farmer went out to sow his seed. As he was scattering the seed, some fell along the path, and the birds came and ate it up. Some fell on rocky places, where it did not have much soil. It sprang up quickly, because the soil was shallow. But when the sun came up, the plants were scorched, and they withered because they had no root. Other seed fell among thorns, which grew up and choked the plants, so that they did not bear grain. Still other seed fell on good soil. It came up, grew and produced a crop, some multiplying thirty, some sixty, some a hundred times."

Then Jesus said, "Whoever has ears to hear, let them hear."

When he was alone, the Twelve and the others around him asked him about the parables. He told them, "The secret of the kingdom of God has been given to you. But to those on the outside everything is said in parables so that,

> "'they may be ever seeing but never perceiving,
>   and ever hearing but never understanding;
>   otherwise they might turn and be forgiven!'"

Then Jesus said to them, "Don't you understand this parable? How then will you understand any parable? The farmer sows the word. Some people are like seed along the path, where the word is sown. As soon as they hear it, Satan comes and takes away the word that was sown in them. Others, like seed sown on rocky places, hear the word and at once receive it with joy. But since they have no root, they last only a short time. When trouble or persecution comes because of the word, they quickly fall away. Still others, like seed sown among thorns, hear the word; but the worries of this life, the deceitfulness of wealth and the desires for other things come in and choke the word, making it unfruitful. Others, like seed sown on good soil, hear the word, accept it, and produce a crop – some thirty, some sixty, some a hundred times what was sown."

A lamp on a stand

He said to them, "Do you bring in a lamp to put it under a bowl or a bed? Instead, don't you put it on its stand? For whatever is hidden is meant to be disclosed, and whatever is concealed is meant to be brought out into the open. If anyone has ears to hear, let them hear."

"Consider carefully what you hear," he continued. "With the measure you use, it will be measured to you – and even more. Those who have will be given more; as for those who do not have, even what they have will be taken from them."

The parable of the growing seed

He also said, "This is what the kingdom of God is like. A man scatters seed on the ground. Night and day, whether he sleeps or gets up, the seed sprouts and grows, though he does not know how. All by itself the soil produces corn – first the stalk, then the ear, then the full grain in the ear. As soon as the grain is ripe, he puts the sickle to it, because the harvest has come."

The parable of the mustard seed

Again he said, "What shall we say the kingdom of God is like, or what parable shall we use to describe it? It is like a mustard seed, which is the smallest of all seeds on earth. Yet when planted, it grows and becomes the largest of all garden plants, with such big branches that the birds can perch in its shade."

With many similar parables Jesus spoke the word to them, as much as they could understand. He did not say anything to them without using a parable. But when he was alone with his own disciples, he explained everything.

Jesus calms the storm

That day when evening came, he said to his disciples, "Let us go over to the other side. Leaving the crowd behind, they took him along, just as he was, in the boat. There were also other boats with him. A furious squall came up, and the waves broke over the boat, so that it was nearly swamped. Jesus was in the stern, sleeping on a cushion. The disciples woke him and said to him, "Teacher, don't you care if we drown?"

He got up, rebuked the wind and said to the waves, "Quiet! Be still!" Then the wind died down and it was completely calm.

He said to his disciples, "Why are you so afraid? Do you still have no faith?"

They were terrified and asked each other, "Who is this? Even the wind and the waves obey him!"

Jesus restores a demon-possessed man

They went across the lake to the region of the Gerasenes. When Jesus got out of the boat, a man with an evil spirit came from the tombs to meet him. This man lived in the tombs, and no-one could bind him anymore, not even with a chain. For he had often been chained hand and foot, but he tore the chains apart and broke the irons on his feet. No-one was strong enough to subdue him. Night and day among the tombs and in the hills he would cry out and cut himself with stones.

When he saw Jesus from a distance, he ran and fell on his knees in front of him. He shouted at the top of his voice, "What do you want with me, Jesus, Son of the Most High God? In God's name don't torture me!" For Jesus had said to him, "Come out of this man, you evil spirit!"

Then Jesus asked him, "What is your name?"

"My name is Legion," he replied, "for we are many." And he begged Jesus again and again not to send them out of the area.

A large herd of pigs was feeding on the nearby hillside. The demons begged Jesus, "Send us among the pigs; allow us to go into them." He gave them permission, and the evil spirits came out and went into the pigs. The herd, about two thousand in number, rushed down the steep bank into the lake and were drowned.

Those tending the pigs ran off and reported this in the town and countryside, and the people went out to see what had happened. When they came to Jesus, they saw the man who had been possessed by the legion of demons, sitting there, dressed and in his right mind; and they were afraid. Those who had seen it told the people what had happened to the demon-possessed man – and told about the pigs as well. Then the people began to plead with Jesus to leave their region.

As Jesus was getting into the boat, the man who had been demon-possessed begged to go with him. Jesus did not let him, but said, "Go home to your own people and tell them how much the Lord has done for you, and how he has had mercy on you." So the man went away and began to tell in the Decapolis how much Jesus had done for him. And all the people were amazed.

Jesus raises a dead girl and heals a woman who was ill

When Jesus had again crossed over by boat to the other side of the lake, a large crowd gathered round him while he was by the lake. Then one of the synagogue leaders, named Jairus, came, and when he saw Jesus, he fell at his feet. He pleaded earnestly with him, "My little daughter is dying. Please come and put your hands on her so that she will be healed and live." So Jesus went with him.

A large crowd followed and pressed round him. And a woman was there who had been subject to bleeding for twelve years. She had suffered a great deal under the care of many doctors and had spent all she had, yet instead of getting better she grew worse. When she heard about Jesus, she came up behind him in the crowd and touched his cloak, because she thought, "If I just touch his clothes, I will be healed." Immediately her bleeding stopped and she felt in her body that she was freed from her suffering.

At once Jesus realised that power had gone out from him. He

turned round in the crowd and asked, "Who touched my clothes?"

"You see the people crowding against you," his disciples answered, "and yet you can ask, 'Who touched me?' "

But Jesus kept looking around to see who had done it. Then the woman, knowing what had happened to her, came and fell at his feet and, trembling with fear, told him the whole truth. He said to her, "Daughter, your faith has healed you. Go in peace and be freed from your suffering."

While Jesus was still speaking, some people came from the house of Jairus, the synagogue leader. "Your daughter is dead," they said. "Why bother the teacher any more?"

Overhearing what they said, Jesus told him, "Don't be afraid; just believe."

He did not let anyone follow him except Peter, James and John the brother of James. When they came to the home of the synagogue leader, Jesus saw a commotion, with people crying and wailing loudly. He went in and said to them, "Why all this commotion and wailing? The child is not dead but asleep." But they laughed at him.

After he put them all out, he took the child's father and mother and the disciples who were with him, and went in where the child was. He took her by the hand and said to her, "*Talitha koum!* " (which means, "Little girl, I say to you, get up!"). Immediately the girl stood up and began to walk around (she was twelve years old). At this they were completely astonished. He gave strict orders not to let anyone know about this, and told them to give her something to eat.

A prophet without honour

Jesus left there and went to his home town, accompanied by his disciples. When the Sabbath came, he began to teach in the synagogue, and many who heard him were amazed.

"Where did this man get these things?" they asked. "What's this wisdom that has been given him? What are these remarkable miracles he is performing? Isn't this the carpenter? Isn't this

Mary's son and the brother of James, Joseph, Judas and Simon? Aren't his sisters here with us?" And they took offence at him.

Jesus said to them, "Only in their own towns, among their relatives and in their own homes are prophets without honour." He could not do any miracles there, except lay his hands on a few people who were ill and heal them. He was amazed at their lack of faith.

Jesus sends out the Twelve

Then Jesus went around teaching from village to village. Calling the Twelve to him, he began to send them out two by two and gave them authority over evil spirits.

These were his instructions: "Take nothing for the journey except a staff – no bread, no bag, no money in your belts. Wear sandals but not an extra shirt. Whenever you enter a house, stay there until you leave that town. And if any place will not welcome you or listen to you, shake the dust off your feet when you leave, as a testimony against them."

They went out and preached that people should repent. They drove out many demons and anointed with oil many people who were ill and healed them.

John the Baptist beheaded

King Herod heard about this, for Jesus' name had become well known. Some were saying, "John the Baptist has been raised from the dead, and that is why miraculous powers are at work in him."

Others said, "He is Elijah."

And still others claimed, "He is a prophet, like one of the prophets of long ago."

But when Herod heard this, he said, "John, whom I beheaded, has been raised from the dead!"

For Herod himself had given orders to have John arrested, and he had him bound and put in prison. He did this because of Herodias, his brother Philip's wife, whom he had married. For

John had been saying to Herod, "It is not lawful for you to have your brother's wife." So Herodias nursed a grudge against John and wanted to kill him. But she was not able to, because Herod feared John and protected him, knowing him to be a righteous and holy man. When Herod heard John, he was greatly puzzled; yet he liked to listen to him.

Finally the opportune time came. On his birthday Herod gave a banquet for his high officials and military commanders and the leading men of Galilee. When the daughter of Herodias came in and danced, she pleased Herod and his dinner guests.

The king said to the girl, "Ask me for anything you want, and I'll give it to you." And he promised her with an oath, "Whatever you ask I will give you, up to half my kingdom."

She went out and said to her mother, "What shall I ask for?"

"The head of John the Baptist," she answered.

At once the girl hurried in to the king with the request: "I want you to give me right now the head of John the Baptist on a platter."

The king was greatly distressed, but because of his oaths and his dinner guests, he did not want to refuse her. So he immediately sent an executioner with orders to bring John's head. The man went, beheaded John in the prison, and brought back his head on a platter. He presented it to the girl, and she gave it to her mother. On hearing of this, John's disciples came and took his body and laid it in a tomb.

Jesus feeds the five thousand

The apostles gathered round Jesus and reported to him all they had done and taught. Then, because so many people were coming and going that they did not even have a chance to eat, he said to them, "Come with me by yourselves to a quiet place and get some rest."

So they went away by themselves in a boat to a solitary place. But many who saw them leaving recognised them and ran on foot from all the towns and got there ahead of them. When Jesus landed and saw a large crowd, he had compassion on them, because they were like sheep without a shepherd. So he began teaching them many things.

By this time it was late in the day, so his disciples came to him. "This is a remote place," they said, "and it's already very late. Send the people away so that they can go to the surrounding countryside and villages and buy themselves something to eat."

But he answered, "You give them something to eat."

They said to him, "That would take eight months of a man's wages! Are we to go and spend that much on bread and give it to them to eat?"

"How many loaves do you have?" he asked. "Go and see."

When they found out, they said, "Five – and two fish."

Then Jesus told them to make all the people sit down in groups on the green grass. So they sat down in groups of hundreds and fifties. Taking the five loaves and the two fish and looking up to heaven, he gave thanks and broke the loaves. Then he gave them to his disciples to set before the people. He also divided the two fish among them all. They all ate and were satisfied, and the disciples picked up twelve basketfuls of broken pieces of bread and fish. The number of the men who had eaten was five thousand.

Jesus walks on the water

Immediately Jesus made his disciples get into the boat and go on ahead of him to Bethsaida, while he dismissed the crowd. After leaving them, he went up on a mountainside to pray.

When evening came, the boat was in the middle of the lake, and he was alone on land. He saw the disciples straining at the oars, because the wind was against them. Shortly before dawn he went out to them, walking on the lake. He was about to pass by them, but when they saw him walking on the lake, they thought he was a ghost. They cried out, because they all saw him and were terrified.

Immediately he spoke to them and said, "Take courage! It is I. Don't be afraid." Then he climbed into the boat with them, and the wind died down. They were completely amazed, for they had not understood about the loaves; their hearts were hardened.

When they had crossed over, they landed at Gennesaret and anchored there. As soon as they got out of the boat, people recognised Jesus. They ran throughout that whole region and carried those who were ill on mats to wherever they heard he was. And wherever he went – into villages, towns or countryside – they placed those who were ill in the market-places. They begged him to let them touch even the edge of his cloak, and all who touched him were healed.

That which defiles you

The Pharisees and some of the teachers of the law who had come from Jerusalem gathered round Jesus and saw some of his disciples eating food with hands that were defiled, that is, unwashed. (The Pharisees and all the Jews do not eat unless they give their hands a ceremonial washing, holding to the tradition of the elders. When they come from the market-place they do not eat unless they wash. And they observe many other traditions, such as the washing of cups, pitchers and kettles.)

So the Pharisees and teachers of the law asked Jesus, "Why don't your disciples live according to the tradition of the elders instead of eating their food with defiled hands?"

> ### That which defiles you
> ### (Mark 7:1–23)
> The infamous outlaw Jesse James killed a man in a bank robbery and shortly afterward was baptised in Kearney Baptist Church in the USA. Then he killed another man, a bank cashier, and joined the church choir and taught hymn-singing. Apparently Jesse loved Sundays, but didn't always have the time to attend church, as Sunday was the day he robbed trains! Hypocrisy is a terrible thing, and Jesus hated it, particularly when it came from the direction of the religious establishment.

He replied, "Isaiah was right when he prophesied about you hypocrites; as it is written:

> "'These people honour me with their lips,
>   but their hearts are far from me.
> They worship me in vain;
>   their teachings are merely human rules.'

You have let go of the commands of God and are holding on to human traditions."

And he continued, "You have a fine way of setting aside the commands of God in order to observe your own traditions! For Moses said, 'Honour your father and your mother,' and, 'Anyone who curses their father or mother must be put to death.' But you say that if anyone declares that what might have been used to help their father or mother is Corban (that is, devoted to God) – then you no longer let them do anything for their father or mother. Thus you nullify the word of God by your tradition that you have handed down. And you do many things like that."

Again Jesus called the crowd to him and said, "Listen to me, everyone, and understand this. Nothing outside you can defile you by going into you. Rather, it is what comes out of you that defiles you."

After he had left the crowd and entered the house, his disciples asked him about this parable. "Are you so dull?" he asked. "Don't you see that nothing that enters you from the outside can defile you? For it doesn't go into your heart but into your stomach, and then out of your body." (In saying this, Jesus declared all foods clean.)

He went on: "What comes out of you is what defiles you. For from within, out of your hearts, come evil thoughts, sexual immorality, theft, murder, adultery, greed, malice, deceit, lewdness, envy, slander, arrogance and folly. All these evils come from inside and defile you."

Jesus honours a Syro-Phoenician woman's faith

Jesus left that place and went to the vicinity of Tyre. He entered a house and did not want anyone to know it; yet he could not keep his presence secret. In fact, as soon as she heard about him, a woman whose little daughter was possessed by an evil spirit came and fell at his feet. The woman was a Greek, born in Syrian Phoenicia. She begged Jesus to drive the demon out of her daughter.

"First let the children eat all they want," he told her, "for it is not right to take the children's bread and toss it to the dogs."

"Lord," she replied, "even the dogs under the table eat the children's crumbs."

Then he told her, "For such a reply, you may go; the demon has left your daughter."

The faith of the Syro-Phoenician woman (Mark 7:24–30)

The sick little girl's mother was a Gentile, a non-Jew. Jesus' mission at this time was to Israel and the Jews.

After his death and resurrection the gospel, or good news, was to be for everyone, but not now. Gentile evangelism was not a top priority at this stage. The woman knew this too, but her faith was unrelenting. Jesus answered her prayer and her daughter was healed.

She went home and found her child lying on the bed, and the demon gone.

Jesus heals a deaf and mute man

Then Jesus left the vicinity of Tyre and went through Sidon, down to the Sea of Galilee and into the region of the Decapolis. There some people brought to him a man who was deaf and could hardly talk, and they begged Jesus to place his hand on him.

After he took him aside, away from the crowd, Jesus put his fingers into the man's ears. Then he spat and touched the man's tongue. He looked up to heaven and with a deep sigh said to him, *"Ephphatha!"* (which means, "Be opened!"). At this, the man's ears were opened, his tongue was loosed and he began to speak plainly.

Jesus commanded them not to tell anyone. But the more he did so, the more they kept talking about it. People were overwhelmed with amazement. "He has done everything well," they said. "He even makes the deaf hear and the mute speak."

Jesus feeds the four thousand

During those days another large crowd gathered. Since they had nothing to eat, Jesus called his disciples to him and said, "I have compassion for these people; they have already been with me three days and have nothing to eat. If I send them home hungry, they will collapse on the way, because some of them have come a long distance."

His disciples answered, "But where in this remote place can anyone get enough bread to feed them?"

"How many loaves do you have?" Jesus asked.

"Seven," they replied.

He told the crowd to sit down on the ground. When he had taken the seven loaves and given thanks, he broke them and gave them to his disciples to set before the people, and they did so. They had a few small fish as well; he gave thanks for them also and told the disciples to distribute them. The people ate and were satisfied. Afterwards the disciples picked up seven basketfuls of broken pieces that were left over. About four thousand were present. And having sent them away, he got into the boat with his disciples and went to the region of Dalmanutha.

The Pharisees came and began to question Jesus. To test him, they asked him for a sign from heaven. He sighed deeply and said, "Why does this generation ask for a sign? Truly I tell you, no sign will be given to it." Then he left them, got back into the boat and crossed to the other side.

The yeast of the Pharisees and Herod

The disciples had forgotten to bring bread, except for one loaf they had with them in the boat. "Be careful," Jesus warned them. "Watch out for the yeast of the Pharisees and that of Herod."

They discussed this with one another and said, "It is because we have no bread."

Aware of their discussion, Jesus asked them: "Why are you talking about having no bread? Do you still not see or understand? Are your hearts hardened? Do you have eyes but fail to see, and ears but fail to hear? And don't you remember? When I broke the five loaves for the five thousand, how many basketfuls of pieces did you pick up?"

"Twelve," they replied.

"And when I broke the seven loaves for the four thousand, how many basketfuls of pieces did you pick up?"

They answered, "Seven."

He said to them, "Do you still not understand?"

Jesus heals a blind man at Bethsaida

They came to Bethsaida, and some people brought a blind man and begged Jesus to touch him. He took the blind man by the hand and led him outside the village. When he had spat on the man's eyes and put his hands on him, Jesus asked, "Do you see anything?"

He looked up and said, "I see people; they look like trees walking around."

Once more Jesus put his hands on the man's eyes. Then his eyes were opened, his sight was restored, and he saw everything clearly. Jesus sent him home, saying, "Don't even go into the village."

Peter declares that Jesus is the Messiah

Jesus and his disciples went on to the villages around Caesarea Philippi. On the way he asked them, "Who do people say I am?"

They replied, "Some say John the Baptist; others say Elijah; and still others, one of the prophets."

"But what about you?" he asked. "Who do you say I am?"

Peter answered, "You are the Messiah."

Jesus warned them not to tell anyone about him.

Jesus predicts his death

He then began to teach them that the Son of Man must suffer many things and be rejected by the elders, the chief priests and the teachers of the law, and that he must be killed and after three days rise again. He spoke plainly about this, and Peter took him aside and began to rebuke him.

But when Jesus turned and looked at his disciples, he rebuked Peter. "Get behind me, Satan!" he said. "You do not have in mind the concerns of God, but merely human concerns."

The way of the cross

Then he called the crowd to him along with his disciples and said: "Those who would be my disciples must deny themselves and take up their cross and follow me. For those who want to save their life will lose it, but those who lose their life for me and for the gospel will save it. What good is it for you to gain the whole world, yet forfeit your soul? Or what can you give in exchange for your

> **Peter declares that Jesus is the Messiah (Mark 8:27–30)**
>
> Jesus' disciples had been with him for quite a while, and he'd given them plenty of hints as to who he was, though none of them had really grasped the fact that he was the Son of God. But now, almost miraculously, Peter the fisherman's eyes are opened, the penny drops, and he finally realises who Jesus is. He utters his confession with awesome wonder: "You are the Messiah."

soul? If any of you are ashamed of me and my words in this adulterous and sinful generation, the Son of Man will be ashamed of you when he comes in his Father's glory with the holy angels."

And he said to them, "Truly I tell you, some who are standing here will not taste death before they see that the kingdom of God has come with power."

The transfiguration

After six days Jesus took Peter, James and John with him and led them up a high mountain, where they were all alone. There he was transfigured before them. His clothes became dazzling white, whiter than anyone in the world could bleach them. And there appeared before them Elijah and Moses, who were talking with Jesus.

Peter said to Jesus, "Rabbi, it is good for us to be here. Let us put up three shelters – one for you, one for Moses and one for Elijah." (He did not know what to say, they were so frightened.)

Then a cloud appeared and covered them, and a voice came from the cloud: "This is my Son, whom I love. Listen to him!"

Suddenly, when they looked around, they no longer saw anyone with them except Jesus.

As they were coming down the mountain, Jesus gave them orders not to tell anyone what they had seen until the Son of Man had risen from the dead. They kept the matter to

> **The transfiguration (Mark 9:2–23)**
>
> Jesus chose three of his closest friends to spend quality time with, 9,000 feet up Mount Hermon. The transfiguration was a confirmation of Peter's earlier confession that Jesus was the Christ. It really was quite a sight as Jesus' clothes shone brightly, and Elijah and Moses who had been dead for hundreds of years suddenly appeared too! This supernatural occurrence proved to the select group once again who Jesus was, and prepared them for the hard road that lay ahead.

themselves, discussing what "rising from the dead" meant.

And they asked him, "Why do the teachers of the law say that Elijah must come first?"

Jesus replied, "To be sure, Elijah does come first, and restores all things. Why then is it written that the Son of Man must suffer much and be rejected? But I tell you, Elijah has come, and they have done to him everything they wished, just as it is written about him."

Jesus heals a demon-possessed boy

When they came to the other disciples, they saw a large crowd around them and the teachers of the law arguing with them. As soon as all the people saw Jesus, they were overwhelmed with wonder and ran to greet him.

"What are you arguing with them about?" he asked.

A man in the crowd answered, "Teacher, I brought you my son, who is possessed by a spirit that has robbed him of speech. Whenever it seizes him, it throws him to the ground. He foams at the mouth, gnashes his teeth and becomes rigid. I asked your disciples to drive out the spirit, but they could not."

"You unbelieving generation," Jesus replied, "how long shall I stay with you? How long shall I put up with you? Bring the boy to me."

So they brought him. When the spirit saw Jesus, it immediately threw the boy into a convulsion. He fell to the ground and rolled around, foaming at the mouth.

Jesus asked the boy's father, "How long has he been like this?"

> **Jesus heals a demon-possessed boy**
> **(Mark 9:14–29)**
> I've seen first-hand clear cases of young people affected by demonic and evil powers who have manifested strange behaviour. The occult, seances, ouija boards and the like are not to be messed with! This seemed to be the case in this instance. Jesus spoke his words of command and the evil spirit came out of the boy.

"From childhood," he answered. "It has often thrown him into fire or water to kill him. But if you can do anything, take pity on us and help us."

"'If you can'?" said Jesus. "Everything is possible for one who believes."

Immediately the boy's father exclaimed, "I do believe; help me overcome my unbelief!"

When Jesus saw that a crowd was running to the scene, he rebuked the evil spirit. "You deaf and mute spirit," he said, "I command you, come out of him and never enter him again."

The spirit shrieked, convulsed him violently and came out. The boy looked so much like a corpse that many said, "He's dead." But Jesus took him by the hand and lifted him to his feet, and he stood up.

After Jesus had gone indoors, his disciples asked him privately, "Why couldn't we drive it out?"

He replied, "This kind can come out only by prayer."

Jesus predicts his death a second time

They left that place and passed through Galilee. Jesus did not want anyone to know where they were, because he was teaching his disciples. He said to them, "The Son of Man is going to be delivered over to human hands. He will be killed, and after three days he will rise." But they did not understand what he meant and were afraid to ask him about it.

They came to Capernaum. When he was in the house, he asked them, "What were you arguing about on the road?" But they kept quiet because on the way they had argued about who was the greatest.

Sitting down, Jesus called the Twelve and said, "Anyone who wants to be first must be the very last, and the servant of all."

He took a little child whom he placed among them. Taking the child in his arms, he said to them, "Whoever welcomes one of these little children in my name welcomes me; and whoever welcomes me does not welcome me but the one who sent me."

Whoever is not against us is for us

"Teacher," said John, "we saw someone driving out demons in your name and we told him to stop, because he was not one of us."

"Do not stop him," Jesus said. "No-one who does a miracle in my name can in the next moment say anything bad about me, for whoever is not against us is for us. Truly I tell you, anyone who gives you a cup of water in my name because you belong to the Messiah will certainly be rewarded.

Causing to stumble

"If anyone causes one of these little ones – those who believe in me – to stumble, it would be better for them if a large millstone were hung round their neck and they were thrown into the sea. If your hand causes you to stumble, cut it off. It is better for you to enter life maimed than with two hands to go into hell, where the fire never goes out. And if your foot causes you to stumble, cut it off. It is better for you to enter life crippled than to have two feet and be thrown into hell. And if your eye causes you to stumble, pluck it out. It is better for you to enter the kingdom of God with one eye than to have two eyes and be thrown into hell, where

> "'their worm does not die,
> and the fire is not quenched.'

Everyone will be salted with fire.

"Salt is good, but if it loses its saltiness, how can you make it salty again? Have salt in yourselves, and be at peace with each other."

Divorce

Jesus then left that place and went into the region of Judea and across the Jordan. Again crowds of people came to him, and as was his custom, he taught them.

Some Pharisees came and tested him by asking, "Is it lawful for a man to divorce his wife?"

"What did Moses command you?" he replied.

They said, "Moses permitted a man to write a certificate of divorce and send her away."

"It was because your hearts were hard that Moses wrote you this law," Jesus replied. "But at the beginning of creation God 'made them male and female.' 'For this reason a man will leave his father and mother and be united to his wife, and the two will become one flesh.' So they are no longer two, but one. Therefore what God has joined together, let no-one separate."

When they were in the house again, the disciples asked Jesus about this. He answered, "Anyone who divorces his wife and marries another woman commits adultery against her. And if she divorces her husband and marries another man, she commits adultery."

The little children and Jesus (Mark 10:13-16)

It was the Jewish custom for mothers to bring their children to a distinguished rabbi on their first birthday so he might bless them.

This is what the mothers wanted from Jesus, whom they recognised as someone really special. It may or may not be significant that this story comes directly after the passage about divorce. Maybe Jesus was implying that the care and welfare of children should come first.

The little children and Jesus

People were bringing little children to Jesus for him to touch them, but the disciples rebuked them. When Jesus saw this, he was indignant. He said to them, "Let the little children come to me, and do not hinder them, for the kingdom of God belongs to such as these. Truly I tell you, anyone who will not receive the kingdom of God like a little child will never enter it." And he took the children in his arms, put his hands on them and blessed them.

The rich and the kingdom of God

As Jesus started on his way, a man ran up to him and fell on his knees before him. "Good teacher," he asked, "what must I do to inherit eternal life?"

"Why do you call me good?" Jesus answered. "No-one is good – except God alone. You know the commandments: 'Do not murder, do not commit adultery, do not steal, do not give false testimony, do not defraud, honour your father and mother.'"

"Teacher," he declared, "all these I have kept since I was a boy."

Jesus looked at him and loved him. "One thing you lack," he said. "Go, sell everything you have and give to the poor, and you will have treasure in heaven. Then come, follow me."

At this the man's face fell. He went away sad, because he had great wealth.

Jesus looked round and said to his disciples, "How hard it is for the rich to enter the kingdom of God!"

The disciples were amazed at his words. But Jesus said again, "Children, how hard it is to enter the kingdom of God! It is easier for a camel to go through the eye of a needle than for the rich to enter the kingdom of God."

The disciples were even more amazed, and said to each other, "Who then can be saved?"

Jesus looked at them and said,

> **The rich and the kingdom of God (Mark 10:17–31)**
>
> John Rockefeller, the multimillionaire, said this when asked about his fortune: "I have made many millions, but they have brought me no happiness. I would barter them all for the days I sat on an office stool in Cleveland and counted myself rich on $3 a week." You see, money is not everything. There are other things much more important in life than wads of cash and possessions, and this is what Jesus was trying to teach the rich young man. No-one can buy eternal life, happiness or their way into heaven, it's a free gift from God for those who want it by believing and trusting in Jesus.

"Humanly, this is impossible, but not with God; all things are possible with God."

Then Peter spoke up, "We have left everything to follow you!"

"Truly I tell you," Jesus replied, "no-one who has left home or brothers or sisters or mother or father or children or fields for me and the gospel will fail to receive a hundred times as much in this present age: homes, brothers, sisters, mothers, children and fields – along with persecutions – and in the age to come eternal life. But many who are first will be last, and the last first."

Jesus predicts his death a third time

They were on their way up to Jerusalem, with Jesus leading the way, and the disciples were astonished, while those who followed were afraid. Again he took the Twelve aside and told them what was going to happen to him. "We are going up to Jerusalem," he said, "and the Son of Man will be delivered over to the chief priests and the teachers of the law. They will condemn him to death and will hand him over to the Gentiles, who will mock him and spit on him, flog him and kill him. Three days later he will rise."

The request of James and John

Then James and John, the sons of Zebedee, came to him. "Teacher," they said, "we want you to do for us whatever we ask."

"What do you want me to do for you?" he asked.

They replied, "Let one of us sit at your right and the other at your left in your glory."

"You don't know what you are asking," Jesus said. "Can you drink the cup I drink or be baptised with the baptism I am baptised with?"

"We can," they answered.

Jesus said to them, "You will drink the cup I drink and be baptised with the baptism I am baptised with, but to sit at my right or left is not for me to grant. These places belong to those for whom they have been prepared."

When the ten heard about this, they became indignant with James and John. Jesus called them together and said, "You know that those who are regarded as rulers of the Gentiles lord it over them, and their high officials exercise authority over them. Not so with you. Instead, whoever wants to become great among you must be your servant, and whoever wants to be first must be slave of all. For even the Son of Man did not come to be served, but to serve, and to give his life as a ransom for many."

Blind Bartimaeus receives his sight

Then they came to Jericho. As Jesus and his disciples, together with a large crowd, were leaving the city, a blind man, Bartimaeus (that is, the Son of Timaeus), was sitting by the roadside begging. When he heard that it was Jesus of Nazareth, he began to shout, "Jesus, Son of David, have mercy on me!"

Many rebuked him and told him to be quiet, but he shouted all the more, "Son of David, have mercy on me!"

Jesus stopped and said, "Call him."

So they called to the blind man, "Cheer up! On your feet! He's calling you." Throwing his cloak aside, he jumped to his feet and came to Jesus.

"What do you want me to do for you?" Jesus asked him.

The blind man said, "Rabbi, I want to see."

"Go," said Jesus, "your faith has healed you." Immediately he received his sight and followed Jesus along the road.

Jesus comes to Jerusalem as king

As they approached Jerusalem and came to Bethphage and Bethany at the Mount of Olives, Jesus sent two of his disciples, saying to them, "Go to the village ahead of you, and just as you enter it, you will find a colt tied there, which no-one has ever ridden. Untie it and bring it here. If anyone asks you, 'Why are you doing this?' say, 'The Lord needs it and will send it back here shortly.'"

They went and found a colt outside in the street, tied at a doorway. As they untied it, some people standing there asked, "What are you doing, untying that colt?" They answered as Jesus had told them to, and the people let them go. When they brought the colt to Jesus and threw their cloaks over it, he sat on it. Many people spread their cloaks on the road, while others spread branches they had cut in the fields. Those who went ahead and those who followed shouted,

"Hosanna!"

"Blessed is he who comes in the name of the Lord!"

"Blessed is the coming kingdom of our father David!"

"Hosanna in the highest heaven!"

Jesus entered Jerusalem and went into the temple courts. He looked around at everything, but since it was already late, he went out to Bethany with the Twelve.

Jesus curses a fig-tree and clears the temple courts

The next day as they were leaving Bethany, Jesus was hungry. Seeing in the distance a fig-tree in leaf, he went to find out if it had any fruit. When he reached it, he found nothing but leaves, because it was not the season for figs. Then he said to the tree, "May no-one ever eat fruit from you again." And his disciples heard him say it.

On reaching Jerusalem, Jesus entered the temple courts and began driving out those who were buying and selling there. He overturned the tables of the money-changers and the benches of those selling doves, and would not allow anyone to carry merchandise through the temple courts. And as he taught them, he said, "Is it not written:

"'My house will be called
a house of prayer for all nations'?

But you have made it 'a den of robbers'."

The chief priests and the teachers of the law heard this and began looking for a way to kill him, for they feared him, because the whole crowd was amazed at his teaching.

When evening came, they went out of the city.

In the morning, as they went along, they saw the fig-tree withered from the roots. Peter remembered and said to Jesus, "Rabbi, look! The fig-tree you cursed has withered!"

"Have faith in God," Jesus answered. "Truly I tell you, if you say to this mountain, 'Go, throw yourself into the sea,' and do not doubt in your heart but believe that what you say will happen, it will be done for you. Therefore I tell you, whatever you ask for in prayer, believe that you have received it, and it will be yours. And when you stand praying, if you hold anything against anyone, forgive them, so that your Father in heaven may forgive you your sins."

The authority of Jesus questioned

They arrived again in Jerusalem, and while Jesus was walking in the temple courts, the chief priests, the teachers of the law and the elders came to him. "By what authority are you doing these things?" they asked. "And who gave you authority to do this?"

Jesus replied, "I will ask you one question. Answer me, and I will tell you by what authority I am doing these things. John's baptism – was it from heaven, or of human origin? Tell me!"

They discussed it among themselves and said, "If we say, 'From heaven', he will ask, 'Then why didn't you believe him?' But if we say, 'Of human origin' . . ." (They feared the people, for everyone held that John really was a prophet.)

So they answered Jesus, "We don't know."

Jesus said, "Neither will I tell you by what authority I am doing these things."

The parable of the tenants

He then began to speak to them in parables: "A man planted a vineyard. He put a wall round it, dug a pit for the winepress and built a watchtower. Then he rented the vineyard to some farmers and moved to another place. At harvest time he sent a servant to the tenants to collect from them some of the fruit of the vineyard. But they seized him, beat him and sent him away empty-handed. Then he sent another servant to them; they struck this man on the head and treated him shamefully. He sent still another, and that one they killed. He sent many others; some of them they beat, others they killed.

"He had one left to send, a son, whom he loved. He sent him last of all, saying, 'They will respect my son.'

"But the tenants said to one another, 'This is the heir. Come, let's kill him, and the inheritance will be ours.' So they took him and killed him, and threw him out of the vineyard.

"What then will the owner of the vineyard do? He will come and kill those tenants and give the vineyard to others. Haven't you read this passage of Scripture:

> "'The stone the builders rejected
>   has become the cornerstone;
> the Lord has done this,
>   and it is marvellous in our eyes'?"

Then the chief priests, the teachers of the law and the elders looked for a way to arrest him because they knew he had spoken the parable against them. But they were afraid of the crowd; so they left him and went away.

Paying the poll-tax to Caesar

Later they sent some of the Pharisees and Herodians to Jesus to catch him in his words. They came to him and said, "Teacher, we know that you are a man of integrity. You aren't swayed by others, because you pay no attention to who they are; but you teach the way of God in accordance with the truth. Is it right to pay the poll-tax to Caesar or not? Should we pay or shouldn't we?"

But Jesus knew their hypocrisy. "Why are you trying to trap me?" he asked. "Bring me a denarius and let me look at it." They brought the coin, and he asked them, "Whose portrait is this? And whose inscription?"

"Caesar's," they replied.

Then Jesus said to them, "Give back to Caesar what is Caesar's and to God what is God's."

And they were amazed at him.

Marriage at the resurrection

Then the Sadducees, who say there is no resurrection, came to him with a question. "Teacher," they said,

---

Paying the poll-tax to Caesar (Mark 12:13–17)

They say two things are inevitable in life: death and taxes! In Jesus' day the taxation system was very complex. All men and women had to pay a poll tax for just existing. Then there was a ground tax of one tenth of all grain grown, and one fifth of wine and oil; and then income tax of 1 per cent. A tax was payable for using the main roads, harbours and markets. There was also a tax on a cart, on each wheel of it, and on the animals that drew it. There was a purchase tax on certain articles, and there were import and export duties too . . . and you thought taxes today were complicated!

"Moses wrote for us that if a man's brother dies and leaves a wife but no children, the man must marry the widow and raise up an heir for his brother. Now there were seven brothers. The first one married and died without leaving any children. The second one married the widow, but he also died, leaving no child. It was the same with the third. In fact, none of the seven left any children. Last of all, the woman died too. At the resurrection whose wife will she be, since the seven were married to her?"

Jesus replied, "Are you not in error because you do not know the Scriptures or the power of God? When the dead rise, they will neither marry nor be given in marriage; they will be like the angels in heaven. Now about the dead rising – have you not read in the Book of Moses, in the account of the burning bush, how God said to him, 'I am the God of Abraham, the God of Isaac, and the God of Jacob'? He is not the God of the dead, but of the living. You are badly mistaken!"

The greatest commandment

One of the teachers of the law came and heard them debating. Noticing that Jesus had given them a good answer, he asked him, "Of all the commandments, which is the most important?"

"The most important one," answered Jesus, "is this: 'Hear, O Israel, the Lord our God, the Lord is one. Love the Lord your God with all your heart and with all your soul and with all your mind and with all your strength.' The second is this: 'Love your neighbour as yourself.' There is no commandment greater than these."

"Well said, teacher," the man replied. "You are right in saying that God is one and there is no other but him. To love him with all your heart, with all your understanding and with all your strength, and to love your neighbour as yourself is more important than all burnt offerings and sacrifices."

When Jesus saw that he had answered wisely, he said to him,

"You are not far from the kingdom of God." And from then on no-one dared ask him any more questions.

Whose son is the Messiah?

While Jesus was teaching in the temple courts, he asked, "Why do the teachers of the law say that the Messiah is the son of David? David himself, speaking by the Holy Spirit, declared:

> "'The Lord said to my Lord:
> "Sit at my right hand
> until I put your enemies
> under your feet.'"

David himself calls him 'Lord'. How then can he be his son?"
  The large crowd listened to him with delight.

Warning against the teachers of the law

As he taught, Jesus said, "Watch out for the teachers of the law. They like to walk around in flowing robes and be greeted with respect in the market-places, and have the most important seats in the synagogues and the places of honour at banquets. They devour widows' houses and for a show make lengthy prayers. These men will be punished most severely."

The widow's offering

Jesus sat down opposite the place where the offerings were put and watched the crowd putting their money into the temple treasury. Many rich people threw in large amounts. But a poor widow came and put in two very small copper coins, worth only a fraction of a penny.

  Calling his disciples to him, Jesus said, "Truly I tell you, this poor widow has put more into the treasury than all the others. They all gave out of their wealth; but she, out of her poverty, put in everything – all she had to live on."

The destruction of the temple and signs of the end times

As he was leaving the temple, one of his disciples said to him, "Look, Teacher! What massive stones! What magnificent buildings!"

"Do you see all these great buildings?" replied Jesus. "Not one stone here will be left on another; every one will be thrown down."

As Jesus was sitting on the Mount of Olives opposite the temple, Peter, James, John and Andrew asked him privately, "Tell us, when will these things happen? And what will be the sign that they are all about to be fulfilled?"

Jesus said to them: "Watch out that no-one deceives you. Many will come in my name, claiming, 'I am he,' and will deceive many. When you hear of wars and rumours of wars, do not be alarmed. Such things must happen, but the end is still to come. Nation will rise against nation, and kingdom against kingdom. There will be earthquakes in various places, and famines. These are the beginning of birth-pains.

"You must be on your guard. You will be handed over to the local councils and flogged in the synagogues. On account of me you will stand before governors and kings as witnesses to them. And the gospel must first be preached to all nations. Whenever you are arrested and brought to trial, do not worry beforehand about what to say. Just say whatever is given you at the time, for it is not you speaking, but the Holy Spirit.

"Brother will betray brother to death, and a father his child. Children will rebel against their parents and have them put to death. Everyone will hate you because of me, but those who stand firm to the end will be saved.

"When you see 'the abomination that causes desolation' standing where it does not belong – let the reader understand – then let those who are in Judea flee to the mountains. Let no-one on the housetop go down or enter the house to take anything out. Let no-one in the field go back to get their cloak. How dreadful it will be in those days for pregnant women and nursing mothers! Pray that this will not take place in winter, because those will be days of distress unequalled from the beginning, when God created the world, until now – and never to be equalled again.

"If the Lord had not cut short those days, no-one would survive. But for the sake of the elect, whom he has chosen, he has shortened them. At that time if anyone says to you, 'Look, here is the Messiah!' or, 'Look, there he is!' do not believe it. For false messiahs and false prophets will appear and perform signs and wonders to deceive, if possible, even the elect. So be on your guard; I have told you everything in advance.

"But in those days, following that distress,

> "'the sun will be darkened,
>   and the moon will not give its light;
> the stars will fall from the sky,
>   and the heavenly bodies will be shaken.'

"At that time people will see the Son of Man coming in clouds with great power and glory. And he will send his angels and gather his elect from the four winds, from the ends of the earth to the ends of the heavens.

"Now learn this lesson from the fig-tree: As soon as its twigs become tender and its leaves come out, you know that summer is near. Even so, when you see these things happening, you know that it is near, right at the door. Truly I tell you, this generation will certainly not pass away until all these things have happened. Heaven and earth will pass away, but my words will never pass away.

The day and hour unknown

"But about that day or hour no-one knows, not even the angels in heaven, nor the Son, but only the Father. Be on guard! Be alert! You do not know when that time will come. It's like a man going away: He leaves his house and puts his servants in charge, each with an assigned task, and tells the one at the door to keep watch.

"Therefore keep watch because you do not know when the owner of the house will come back – whether in the evening, or at midnight, or when the cock crows, or at dawn. If he comes suddenly, do not let him find you sleeping. What I say to you, I say to everyone: 'Watch!'"

Jesus anointed at Bethany

Now the Passover and the Feast of Unleavened Bread were only two days away, and the chief priests and the teachers of the law were looking for some sly way to arrest Jesus and kill him. "But not during the Feast," they said, "or the people may riot."

While he was in Bethany, reclining at the table in the home of Simon the Leper, a woman came with an alabaster jar of very expensive perfume, made of pure nard. She broke the jar and poured the perfume on his head.

Some of those present were saying indignantly to one another, "Why this waste of perfume? It could have been sold for more than a year's wages and the money given to the poor." And they rebuked her harshly.

"Leave her alone," said Jesus. "Why are you bothering her? She has done a beautiful thing to me. The poor you will always have with you, and you can help them any time you want. But you will not always have me. She did what she could. She poured perfume on my body beforehand to prepare for my burial. Truly I tell you, wherever the gospel is preached throughout the world, what she has done will also be told, in memory of her."

Then Judas Iscariot, one of the Twelve, went to the chief priests to betray Jesus to them. They were delighted to hear this and promised to give him money. So he watched for an opportunity to hand him over.

The Lord's Supper

On the first day of the Feast of Unleavened Bread, when it was customary to sacrifice the Passover lamb, Jesus' disciples asked him, "Where do you want us to go and make preparations for you to eat the Passover?"

So he sent two of his disciples, telling them, "Go into the city, and a man carrying a jar of water will meet you. Follow him. Say to the owner of the house he enters, 'The Teacher asks: Where is my guest room, where I may eat the Passover with my disciples?' He will show you a large room upstairs, furnished and ready. Make preparations for us there."

The disciples left, went into the city and found things just as Jesus had told them. So they prepared the Passover.

When evening came, Jesus arrived with the Twelve. While they were reclining at the table eating, he said, "Truly I tell you, one of you will betray me – one who is eating with me."

They were saddened, and one by one they said to him, "Surely not I?"

> **The Lord's Supper**
> **(Mark 14:12–26)**
> Jesus' extraordinary life was about to come to an end. Whilst he was in Bethany, the Sanhedrin (the Jewish court) was meeting in the High Priest's palace to arrange for his arrest and execution. Jesus knew his mission was nearing its end, and so he wanted to spend his last days with his friends. He arranged a meal, which has become known as The Last Supper, where they sat and ate yeast-free bread and drank red wine together.

"It is one of the Twelve," he replied, "one who dips bread into the bowl with me. The Son of Man will go just as it is written about him. But woe to that man who betrays the Son of Man! It would be better for him if he had not been born."

While they were eating, Jesus took bread, and when he had given thanks, he broke it and gave it to his disciples, saying, "Take it; this is my body."

Then he took the cup, and when he had given thanks, he gave it to them, and they all drank from it.

"This is my blood of the covenant, which is poured out for many," he said to them. "Truly I tell you, I will not drink again of the fruit of the vine until that day when I drink it new in the kingdom of God."

When they had sung a hymn, they went out to the Mount of Olives.

Jesus predicts Peter's denial

"You will all fall away," Jesus told them, "for it is written:

> "*I will strike the shepherd,*
> *and the sheep will be scattered.'*

But after I have risen, I will go ahead of you into Galilee."

Peter declared, "Even if all fall away, I will not."

"Truly I tell you," Jesus answered, "today – yes, tonight – before the cock crows twice you yourself will disown me three times."

But Peter insisted emphatically, "Even if I have to die with you, I will never disown you." And all the others said the same.

Gethsemane

They went to a place called Gethsemane, and Jesus said to his disciples, "Sit here while I pray." He took Peter, James and John along with him, and he began to be deeply distressed and troubled. "My soul is overwhelmed with sorrow to the point of death," he said to them. "Stay here and keep watch."

Going a little farther, he fell to the ground and prayed that if possible the hour might pass from him. "*Abba*, Father," he said, "everything is possible for you. Take this cup from me. Yet not what I will, but what you will."

Then he returned to his disciples and found them sleeping. "Simon," he said to Peter, "are you asleep? Could you not keep watch for one hour? Watch and pray so that you will not fall into temptation. The spirit is willing, but the flesh is weak."

Once more he went away and prayed the same thing. When he came back, he again found them sleeping, because their eyes were heavy. They did not know what to say to him.

Returning the third time, he said to them, "Are you still sleeping and resting? Enough! The hour has come. Look, the Son of Man is delivered into the hands of sinners. Rise! Let us go! Here comes my betrayer!"

Jesus arrested

Just as he was speaking, Judas, one of the Twelve, appeared. With him was a crowd armed with swords and clubs, sent from the chief priests, the teachers of the law, and the elders.

Now the betrayer had arranged a signal with them: "The one I kiss is the man; arrest him and lead him away under guard." Going at once to Jesus, Judas said, "Rabbi!" and kissed him. The men seized Jesus and arrested him. Then one of those standing near drew his sword and struck the servant of the high priest, cutting off his ear.

"Am I leading a rebellion," said Jesus, "that you have come out with swords and clubs to capture me? Every day I was with you, teaching in the temple courts, and you did not arrest me. But the Scriptures must be fulfilled." Then everyone deserted him and fled.

A young man, wearing nothing but a linen garment, was following Jesus. When they seized him, he fled naked, leaving his garment behind.

Jesus before the Sanhedrin

They took Jesus to the high priest, and all the chief priests, the elders and the teachers of the law came together. Peter followed him at a distance, right into the courtyard of the high priest. There he sat with the guards and warmed himself at the fire.

The chief priests and the whole Sanhedrin were looking for evidence against Jesus so that they could put him to death, but they did not find any. Many testified falsely against him, but their statements did not agree.

Then some stood up and gave this false testimony against him: "We heard him say, 'I will destroy this temple made with human hands and in three days will build another, not made with hands.'" Yet even then their testimony did not agree.

Then the high priest stood up before them and asked Jesus, "Are you not going to answer? What is this testimony that these men are bringing against you?" But Jesus remained silent and gave no answer.

Again the high priest asked him, "Are you the Messiah, the Son of the Blessed One?"

"I am," said Jesus. "And you will see the Son of Man sitting at the right hand of the Mighty One and coming on the clouds of heaven."

The high priest tore his clothes. "Why do we need any more witnesses?" he asked. "You have heard the blasphemy. What do you think?"

They all condemned him as worthy of death. Then some began to spit at him; they blindfolded him, struck him with their fists, and said, "Prophesy!" And the guards took him and beat him.

Peter disowns Jesus

While Peter was below in the courtyard, one of the servant-girls of the high priest came by. When she saw Peter warming himself, she looked closely at him.

"You also were with that Nazarene, Jesus," she said.

But he denied it. "I don't know or understand what you're talking about," he said, and went out into the entrance.

When the servant-girl saw him there, she said again to those standing round them, "This fellow is one of them." Again he denied it.

After a little while, those standing near said to Peter, "Surely you are one of them, for you are a Galilean."

He began to call down curses, and he swore to them, "I don't know this man you're talking about."

Immediately the cock crowed the second time. Then Peter remembered the word Jesus had spoken to him: "Before the cock crows twice you will disown me three times." And he broke down and wept.

Jesus before Pilate

Very early in the morning, the chief priests, with the elders, the teachers of the law and the whole Sanhedrin, reached a decision. They bound Jesus, led him away and handed him over to Pilate.

"Are you the king of the Jews?" asked Pilate.

"You have said so," Jesus replied.

The chief priests accused him of many things. So again Pilate asked him, "Aren't you going to answer? See how many things they are accusing you of."

But Jesus still made no reply, and Pilate was amazed.

Now it was the custom at the Feast to release a prisoner whom the people requested. A man called Barabbas was in prison with the insurrectionists who had committed murder in the uprising. The crowd came up and asked Pilate to do for them what he usually did.

"Do you want me to release to you the king of the Jews?" asked Pilate, knowing it was out of envy that the chief priests had handed Jesus over to him. But the chief priests stirred up the crowd to get Pilate to release Barabbas instead.

"What shall I do, then, with the one you call the king of the Jews?" Pilate asked them.

"Crucify him!" they shouted.

"Why? What crime has he committed?" asked Pilate.

But they shouted all the louder, "Crucify him!"

Wanting to satisfy the crowd, Pilate released Barabbas to them. He had Jesus flogged, and handed him over to be crucified.

The soldiers mock Jesus

The soldiers led Jesus away into the palace (that is, the Praetorium) and called together the whole company of soldiers. They put a purple robe on him, then twisted together a crown of thorns and set it on him. And they began to call out to him, "Hail, king of the Jews!" Again and again they struck him on the head with a staff and spat on him. Falling on their knees, they paid homage to him. And when they had mocked him, they took off the purple robe and put his own clothes on him. Then they led him out to crucify him.

The crucifixion

A certain man from Cyrene, Simon, the father of Alexander and Rufus, was passing by on his way in from the country, and they forced him to carry the cross. They brought Jesus to the place called Golgotha (which means The Place of the Skull). Then they offered him wine mixed with myrrh, but he did not take it. And they crucified him. Dividing up his clothes, they cast lots to see what each would get.

It was nine in the morning when they crucified him. The written notice of the charge against him read: THE KING OF THE JEWS.

They crucified two rebels with him, one on his right and one on his left. Those who passed by hurled insults at him, shaking their heads and saying, "So! You who are going to destroy the temple and build it in three days, come down from the cross and save yourself!"

In the same way the chief priests and the teachers of the law mocked him among themselves. "He saved others," they said, "but he can't save himself! Let this Messiah, this king of Israel, come down now from the cross, that we may see and believe." Those crucified with him also heaped insults on him.

The death of Jesus

At noon, darkness came over the whole land until three in the afternoon. And at three in the afternoon Jesus cried out in a loud voice, "*Eloi, Eloi, lema sabachthani?*" – which means, "My God, my God, why have you forsaken me?"

When some of those standing near heard this, they said, "Listen, he's calling Elijah."

Someone ran, filled a sponge with wine vinegar, put it on a staff, and offered it to Jesus to drink. "Now leave him alone. Let's see if Elijah comes to take him down," he said.

With a loud cry, Jesus breathed his last.

The curtain of the temple was torn in two from top to bottom. And when the centurion, who stood there in front of Jesus, saw how he died, he said, "Surely this man was the Son of God!"

The crucifixion
(Mark 15:21–41)

On one occasion the great artist Michelangelo turned to his fellow artists and said with frustration in his voice: "Why do you keep filling gallery after gallery with endless pictures of Christ in weakness, Christ on the cross, and most of all, Christ hanging dead. Why do you concentrate on the passing episode as if the curtain dropped down there on disaster and defeat? That dreadful scene lasted only a few hours. But to the unending eternity Christ is alive, Christ rules and reigns in triumph." The word "crucifixion" means to fasten to a cross. It dates back to 600 BC and was abolished by the Emperor Constantine in AD 337. It was the cruellest and most painful death that has ever been invented by man.

Some women were watching from a distance. Among them were Mary Magdalene, Mary the mother of James the younger and of Joseph, and Salome. In Galilee these women had followed him and cared for his needs. Many other women who had come up with him to Jerusalem were also there.

The burial of Jesus

It was Preparation Day (that is, the day before the Sabbath). So as evening approached, Joseph of Arimathea, a prominent member of the Council, who was himself waiting for the kingdom of God, went boldly to Pilate and asked for Jesus' body. Pilate was surprised to hear that he was already dead. Summoning the centurion, he asked him if Jesus had already died. When he learned from the centurion that it was so, he gave the body to Joseph. So Joseph bought some linen cloth, took down the body, wrapped it in the linen, and placed it in a tomb cut out of rock. Then he rolled a stone against the entrance of the tomb. Mary Magdalene and Mary the mother of Joseph saw where he was laid.

He has risen!

When the Sabbath was over, Mary Magdalene, Mary the mother of James, and Salome bought spices so that they might go to anoint Jesus' body. Very early on the first day of the week, just after sunrise, they were on their way to the tomb and they asked each other, "Who will roll the stone away from the entrance of the tomb?"

But when they looked up, they saw that the stone, which was very large, had been rolled away. As they entered the tomb, they saw a young man dressed in a white robe sitting on the right side, and they were alarmed.

"Don't be alarmed," he said. "You are looking for Jesus the Nazarene, who was crucified. He has risen! He is not here. See the place where they laid him. But go, tell his disciples and Peter, 'He is going ahead of you into Galilee. There you will see him, just as he told you.' "

Trembling and bewildered, the women went out and fled from the tomb. They said nothing to anyone, because they were afraid.

[The following passage is not included in the earliest manuscripts and some other ancient sources.]

When Jesus rose early on the first day of the week, he appeared first to Mary Magdalene, out of whom he had driven seven demons. She went and told those who had been with him and who were mourning and weeping. When they heard that Jesus was alive and that she had seen him, they did not believe it.

Afterwards Jesus appeared in a different form to two of them while they were walking in the country. These returned and reported it to the rest; but they did not believe them either.

Later Jesus appeared to the Eleven as they were eating; he rebuked them for their lack of faith and their stubborn refusal to believe those who had seen him after he had risen.

He said to them, "Go into all the world and preach the gospel to all creation. Whoever believes and is baptised will be saved, but whoever does not believe will be condemned. And these signs will accompany those who believe: In my name they will drive out demons; they will speak in new tongues; they will pick up snakes with their hands; and when they drink deadly poison, it will not hurt them at all; they will place their hands on people who are ill, and they will get well."

After the Lord Jesus had spoken to them, he was taken up into heaven and he sat at the right hand of God. Then the disciples went out and preached everywhere, and the Lord worked with them and confirmed his word by the signs that accompanied it.

RESURRECTION
by Steve Legg

Whilst writing my book, *Man, Myth or Maybe More?*, I wrote to a whole host of well-known personalities, including prime ministers, presidents and royalty to ask their opinions on who they thought Jesus was.

One of the most interesting views came from Claire Rayner, the popular agony aunt, who offered a contribution that she thought I wouldn't like. See what you think: "I find aspects of the worship of Jesus more than a little disturbing. For example, the sadomasochistic nature of the 'Adoration' given to the image of a man bleeding to death while pinned to a cross is a very nasty example of glorification of the sort of human behaviour that is deeply disgusting."

Claire put in her letter that I would probably find this view "very offensive", but in a way I have to totally agree with her. It is rather sick that Christians should worship a man being butchered to death on a cross. We see pictures and stained glass windows in churches the length and breadth of the land. Christians and many others wear crosses around their necks. Could you imagine how weird it might look if people wore miniature sets of gallows around their neck, or electric chair earrings? That would be totally tasteless, wouldn't it?

I believe Claire Rayner is absolutely spot on in her comments, except for the rather major fact that Jesus didn't stay dead. And that is the vital point: Jesus came back to life again. You see, the resurrection of Jesus is the cornerstone of Christianity. The Bible even tells us that if Jesus didn't come back to life then us Christians are wasting our time: "And if Christ has not been raised, your faith is futile" (1 Corinthians 15:17).

Because of his resurrection tragedy turned to triumph.

Jesus offers life, hope and meaning, a destiny and a reason for living, but it really is up to you. What are you going to do with this man Jesus? Are you ready to meet the Millennium Man for yourself? If you are, then this is what you need to do.

Admit
You need to admit that you've done wrong, that you have sinned. Deep down you know that you have gone your own selfish way instead of God's.

Believe
Next you need to believe that Jesus' dying on the cross was the ultimate sacrifice, and made it possible through his death and resurrection for us to start a new life. He paid the price for the death our sins deserve. He carried the can.

Commit
Now it's time for commitment – to commit yourself to living God's way, from this point forward, as a Christian. Remember the advice we often see on all sorts of products we buy in the shops: "For best results, follow the maker's instructions."

Firm Foundations
A Beginner's Guide to Christianity
By Steve Legg

If the Gospel of Mark has inspired you and you would like to discover more about the Christian faith, *Firm Foundations* by Steve Legg should provide just the introduction you need.

It is full of invaluable explanation and guidance on all aspects of the Christian life, and assumes no prior knowledge – it is written both for newcomers to the faith and for those who have not committed themselves but are interested to know more.

By looking at subjects like prayer, the Bible and the Holy Spirit, and lifestyle issues such as money and dealing with temptation, Steve digs deeper into the strong foundations on which Christians build their lives.

Firm Foundations by Steve Legg
£6.99 ISBN: 0 340 86134 7

". . . the word of the Lord endures for ever."

The Gospel of Mark used in this booklet is taken from Today's New International Version, the most recent and up-to-date translation of the Bible.

Today's NIV is based on the world's most popular and respected modern English Bible translation, the New International Version, but has been revised to take into account the latest developments in biblical scholarship and the subtle shifts in use and understanding of our language. The translators' concern has been to ensure the continuing relevance and vibrancy of God's word in the modern world.

Accurate to the original. Relevant to today.

To discover more about Today's NIV, please visit our website: www.hodderbibles.co.uk